D1133908

Rok Oman/Spela Videcnik

Habitation in Extreme Environments

Harvard University
Graduate School of Design

Studio Instructors
Rok Oman, Spela Videcnik

Technology Advisor
Hanif Kara

Workshop Instructors
Hanif Kara, Structure; Klaus Mayer,
Environmental Context; Wolfgang Rieder,
Intelligent Skins

Teaching Associate
Josh Schecter

Students
Myrna Ayoub, Oliver Bucklin, Zheng Cui,
Frederick Kim, Katie MacDonald,
Lauren McClellan, Michael Meo, Erin
Pellegrino, Nadia Perlepe, Elizabeth Pipal,
Tianhang Ren, Xin Su, Elizabeth Wu

Critics
Jamie Blosser, Igor Ekstajn, Simon
Frommenwiler, Lisa Haber-Thomson, Eric
Howeler, Jane Hutton, Mariana Ibañez,
Maria Jaakkola, Hanif Kara, Grace La,
Neil Leach, Klaus Mayer, Ana Miljacki,
Mark Mulligan, Bryan Norwood, Thaddeus
Pawlowski, Camilo Restrepo, Wolfgang
Rieder, Peter Rose, Lola Shepard, Robert
Silman, Felipe Uribe

Introduction

Rok Oman, Spela Videcnik

Extreme climates introduce a design challenge for architects. In a context of harsh environments, it is especially important to design buildings that respond to prevailing conditions—not only as a protective measure but as a benefit for future generations. Given dramatic climate shifts, housing design translates into a matter of immediate life safety for existing populations. In response to these demands, remote settlements in the North must be designed and constructed in accordance with ideas of self-sufficiency and back-up energy systems. Many vernacular building traditions can serve as a reference for designing environments that are holistically sustainable within extreme climatic conditions that challenge comfortable human habitation in the North.

remote terrain introduce ideas of prefabrication and economy of construction within these challenging contexts. Designing inhabitable environments must therefore respond effectively to scarcity, inaccessibility, and unpredictability with innovation particular to extreme climates.

The Harvard University Graduate School of Design sponsored an option studio during the fall of 2014 that dealt with housing in the North. Students questioned and researched traditional European alpine settlements in an attempt to develop new approaches to contemporary architecture within a North American context.

This situation requires incisive designs that respond to irregular loading from strong winds, heavy snowfall, avalanches, and extreme cold. These phenomena are often sudden and unpredictable. Risk of severe weather increases the vulnerability of human habitation to the natural surroundings. The dichotomy between vernacular housing traditions and the latest innovation in building technology establishes an interesting terrain for the design of comfortable living environments. Housing, in particular, must achieve levels of self-sufficiency in such environments to decrease dependency on links to external infrastructure networks that can be severed during periods of harsh weather. At the same time, complications in material provision and inaccessible,

Bivak II, Mojstrana, Na Jezerih, Slovenia, 2012.

Prototype: Slovenia

In the first part of the studio, the design of an inhabitable environment integrated structural and environmental planning considerations with the chosen architectural language of a Slovenian mountain peak. As part of their research, the students traveled to Slovenia to learn from contemporary and vernacular adaptations to a harsh winter climate. They had the opportunity to visit, and even stay in, traditional Slovenian housing. They also met with local designers and fabricators accustomed to working on contemporary adaptations to weather and toured fabrication facilities and job sites.

Task

Challenge

As an introduction to building in these extreme climatic conditions, students were challenged to construct several prototypical designs of a smallest-possible habitable unit using traditional designs that respond to risks associated with avalanches, heavy snowfall, strong winds, and extreme cold. In a series of experiments and tasks, cross-disciplinary tools allowed students to fully comprehend the conditions of their site in an attempt to compile solutions to such a complex design challenge.

The prototype shelter unit had to be designed for easy transportation to its site, low maintenance, and resilience to harsh conditions. The volume was intended to provide shelter for up to eight people for one to three days. The unit was required to offer space for sleeping and cooking and be transportable via helicopter. The weight had to be less than 1,800 kilograms or, if more, the unit had to be transported as a series of smaller parts that could be easily assembled on site. Other challenges included being self-sufficient (without need for external electrical and heating supply networks) and minimizing future maintenance costs. Use of both primitive and vernacular building practices of design involved advanced technology and elements of sustainable architecture (intelligent building skins, etc.) to produce a shelter of no environmental impact within strict design constraints.

Clockwise from top left: Bivak II, Mojstrana, Na Jezerih, Slovenia, 2012. Camp Schurman, Mount Rainier, Washington, 2011. Bivak II, Mojstrana, Na Jezerih, Slovenia, 2012. Denali, Alaska, 2012. Bivak II, Mojstrana, Na Jezerih, Slovenia, 2012. Aljazev Stolp, Mount Triglav, Slovenia, 2008.

A Confined
Technological
Approach

Hanif Kara

A consideration of the many-layered question of "housing" in the short span of a semester, given the role played by many designers and fabricators in this process, is prone to result in credulous and repetitious research, while often falling into the dreamlike ramblings of utopian speculations.

It is also all too easy to fall into a defeatist mindset; in choosing to persevere, this studio attempted to apply a narrow focus to the first half of the semester, setting the challenge of designing prototypes for survival shelters for mountaineers in Slovenia's harsh highlands in a limited timespan, including two short workshops on structure and technology.

Though the subject matter then becomes specific, and the technologies reviewed specialized, such an approach to study has the potential to provide a more reliable output. These research findings can be expanded and applied to other scenarios, helping to tackle the challenges of mass housing in extreme environments that have become prevalent around the globe in recent years.

A notional site was specified and the known constraints tested as part of the prototypical approach. This "production of knowledge"—the learning attached to the process of developing a design through the rigors of construction, facilitating the shift from theory to practice—would be invaluable in the second half of the semester.

There are a great many ways of approaching the task; looking at this through a technological lens, the scenario forces the imagination to move from quickly produced designs for very compact spaces toward more limited distinctions (in terms of its design, methods, and applicability). The studies include fast assembly and erection using helicopters, choosing resilient materials rather than relying on permanence of design, and considering the connections between elements as closely as the elements themselves. We can strive for insulated lightness rather than mass, and views upward to the skies rather than just down to the streets, as well as early application of design and communication tools across disciplines.

In the last two decades, the architectural discipline has had to return to thinking beyond the mere execution of program toward "persuasion by innovation": new types of design intelligence, new technologies, and fascinating forms of fabrication drawn from the digital revolution. Small projects such as this one, or temporary "pavilions" and "pop-ups," have become relevant and prevalent in contemporary design discourse. In this vein, two precedents spring to mind as recognized bases for architectural and artistic experimentation. The first is Black Rock City (originally known as the Burning Man Festival), which takes place annually in the deserts of Nevada; the second is British Antarctic Ice Research Station, Halley VI.

Since its first incarnation in 1986, the Burning Man Festival has produced a number of radical examples of shelters that are built very quickly and leave no trace on the desert. These structures are built to withstand the cold nights and hot days of the arid climate, and to be relatively self-sufficient, since they are used to provide the bare essentials, although located on a fixed plot. Due to the long-term success of

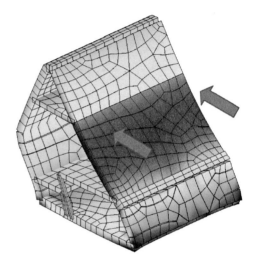

the festivals, which are designed in a C-shaped "city" format, these shelters have been of interest to organizations exploring mass housing such as the United Nations High Commissioner for Refugees, and commercial ventures such as Shelter Systems and World Shelters.

Although many of these concepts have roots in the experimentation of the last century, including those of Buckminster Fuller, more recently some innovative ideas have emerged too. For example, "yurtdomes," the folding ICOSA Pod (a structure based on triangular tensions), or the IKEA-funded flat-packed houses (originally produced for refugees on the Somalia/Ethiopia border by Swedish designer Johan Karlson), have all been tested at this festival.

The Halley VI ice station provides a unique example. Built in 2013 as a mobile permanent

Structural analysis of wind loads on Pop House, the project of Frederick Kim, Katie MacDonald, and Erin Pellegrino.

research center that accommodated the physical, social, and emotional needs of researchers, the station is sited on a massive ice sheet called the Brunt Ice Shelf. It must withstand a brutal climate, with temperatures ranging from -5°C to -50°C. Average snowfall is around 1 meter per year, and there can be total darkness for three months annually.

The First Workshop
In the first group discussion, we drew on the adage that research alone cannot go far enough to define applicable ideas within design and engineering; it is equally important to work with reference to the supply chain in its industrial context.

The compact eight-person prototype would provide a basic survival shelter. Context was important in the design: in terms of scale, it could comprise a two-story "rocky outcrop" within a mountainous landscape, or a stacked "treelike" volume in a field. The themes of construction and transportation in extreme topographies and terrains guided this first discussion, placing particular emphasis on the use of rescue helicopters. This was a methodology pioneered in the early 1900s during the construction of offshore oilrig topside accommodation.

An early understanding of local environmental patterns is crucial to the confined approach. In these more remote areas of Slovenia, this would include a number of extreme acts of nature such as strong winds, fluctuations in temperature, sheet floor ice movement, mudslides, floods, snow drifts, and avalanches. Given the fragility of these conditions, much thought was given to providing lateral and vertical restraint to mountainside accommodation while causing minimal impact on the surrounding land; the geological and orographic features of the site were introduced at this stage.

The opposite was also true: while impact on the mountains would have to be minimal, the ability to withstand—or, more correctly, to divert—the force of an avalanche, should one be triggered, was also a necessity. At their highest speeds, avalanches have been known to obliterate even the strongest reinforced concrete structures, reaching forces of up to 100kN/m^2 (compared to 4kN/m^2 for wind), so the prototypes could not be designed to resist this.

The best alpine architecture, then, is that which develops alternative defense strategies, such as avoiding the known avalanche path altogether, or shaping the design to deflect loads. Given the remote nature of many of these shelters, the considerations that apply to more standard structures are exaggerated here. Adjacent buildings, roads and other infrastructures, gardens, and public spaces can be overlooked, leaving the students to concentrate on purely technical aspects throughout this phase.

The Second Workshop
The second workshop of the studio extended to testing several designs for a variety of load cases, using widely available structural design software to discuss materials, aesthetics, optimization, and integration of each building type. It became apparent that by working through the prototypes together and testing first one that was rocklike and two storys tall, and then another taller design, the whole group could benefit from the analysis. This process worked with key findings from the first workshop, applying these to the designs of each student. Surface structures, framed structures, and braced structures were simulated for the final analysis.

The conclusions drawn were taken into account in the second phase of the semester, with a variety of material options and forms from which to choose. The confined technical approach can also go further in the future to incorporate advanced structural materials alongside the possible use of "drone technologies" for fabrication and installation, which are rapidly developing as an economical option.

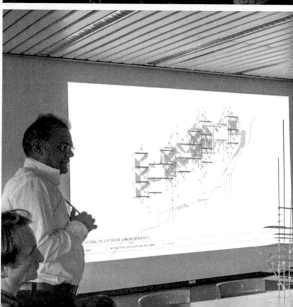

Twin House

Zheng Cui

Twin House is a shelter composed of two modular units. Each module works by itself with the minimum required space and foldable furniture for a group of four people standing, sitting, eating, socializing, and sleeping. Each module unit can be placed in three different positions, creating nine configurations in total for the module assembly, which allows the shelter to adapt to various alpine locations. Five configurations have been tested. Each configuration has a unique indoor and outdoor space character, and varied mountaineering groups could choose different configurations for their use. The two-module system also makes a single module easier for vehicles and a helicopter to deliver to the designated location.

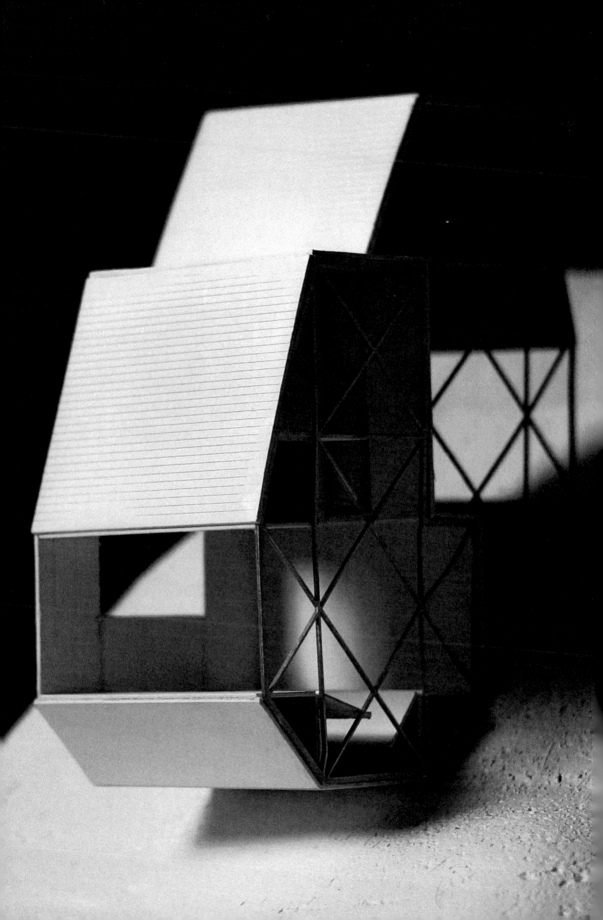

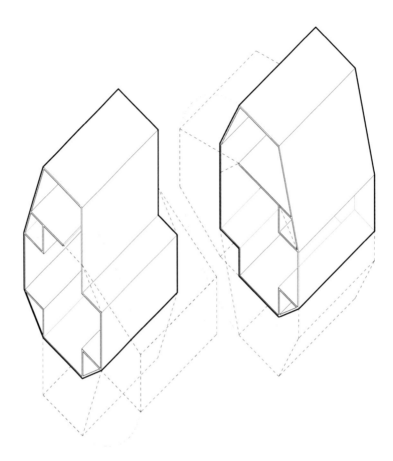

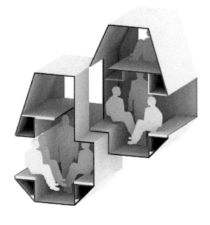

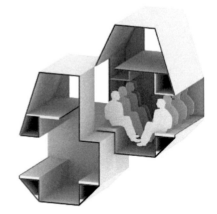

Top: Rotating system.   Bottom: Habitation diagrams.

+4.20

+2.00

+1.70

+1.20

+0.50

0.00

STORAGE

STORAGE

LADDER

STORAGE

STORAGE

STORAGE

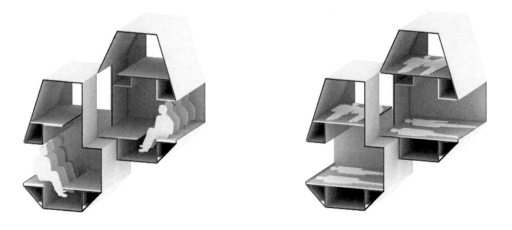

Top: Unit connections.   Bottom: Habitation diagrams.

Ark

Nadia Perlepe

This shelter is conceived as a solid, compact structure with the ability to sustain life in the most extreme of environments, not unlike an ark. This ark|shelter, situated on top of the Slovenian Alps, provides a safe haven for mountaineers at night or in extreme environmental conditions.

The shelter is anchored on the mountain. The interior is organized as an amphitheater, for two reasons. First, the amphitheater is a social space, where hikers sleep, store their belongings, eat, and socialize. Second, the entire *bivak* (a mountain shelter) is a window—a viewing point and observation deck—that opens up to nature and offers views toward both the mountain and the sky. The shelter is a cantilever construction; the amphitheater hangs over the cliff. The separate parts are transported to the site by helicopter and assembled on site.

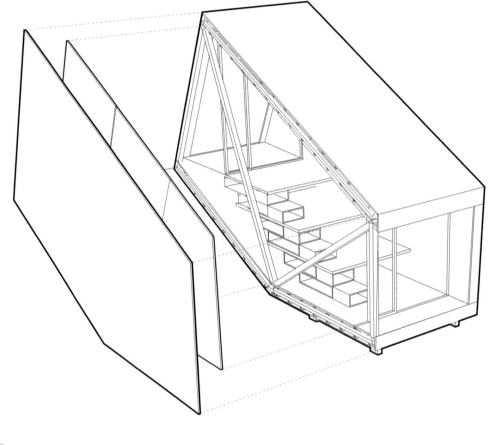

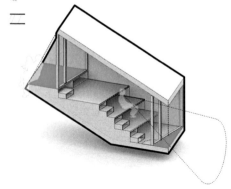

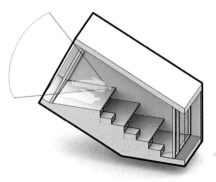

Top: Wall assembly.   Bottom: Views from within.

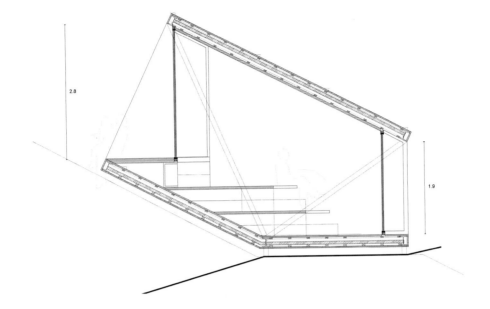

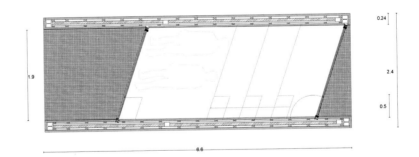

Top: Section.   Bottom: Plan.

Pop House

Frederick Kim
Katie MacDonald
Erin Pellegrino

Pop House is a climbable, modular shelter that adapts to various alpine sites. Deployed by helicopter as a planar assembly, the shelter folds open on site to become a three-dimensional space. The structure's modular system allows for units to be placed along slopes of varying heights. Wooden joints are moved into place and secured with dowels. Inside, beds fold out to accommodate both sleeping and socializing.

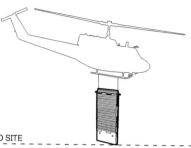

1000 KG - 2.5m x 2.5m - 2 TRIPS TO SITE

1000 KG - 2.5m x 2.5m - 2 TRIPS TO SITE

4000 KG - 5m x 2.5m - 1 TRIPS TO SITE

Deployment strategies.

Frederick Kim, Katie MacDonald, Erin Pellegrino

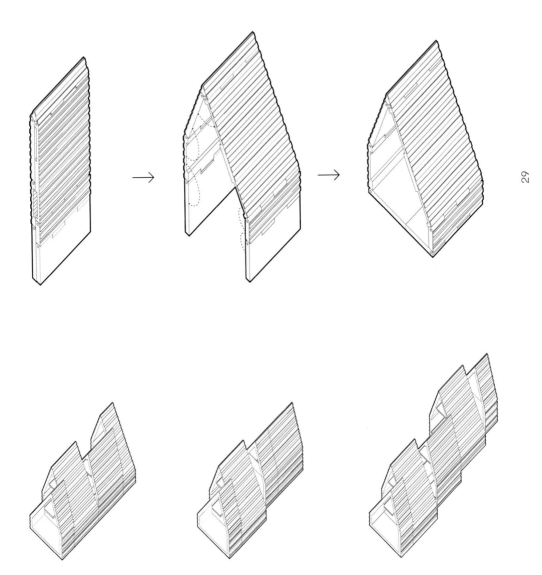

Unfolded assembly.

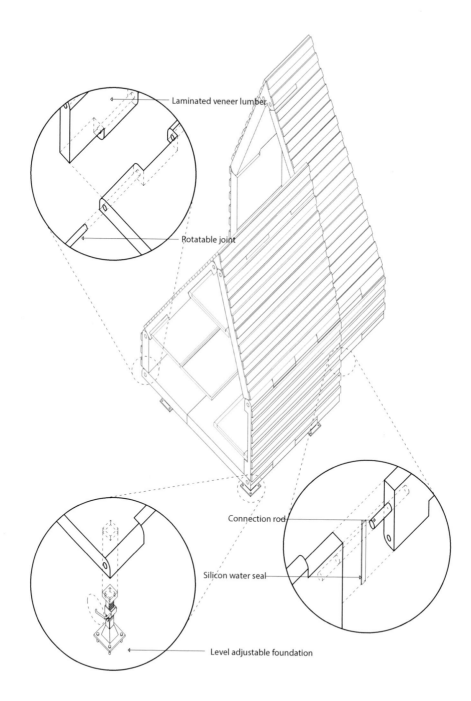

Laminated veneer lumber

Rotatable joint

Connection rod

Silicon water seal

Level adjustable foundation

Module details.

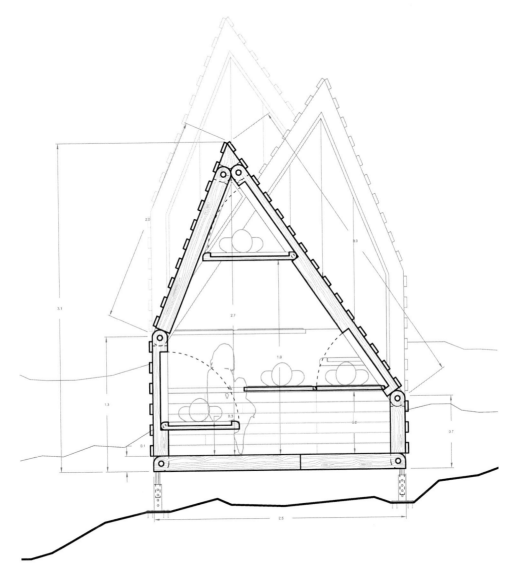

Section.

Operable model.

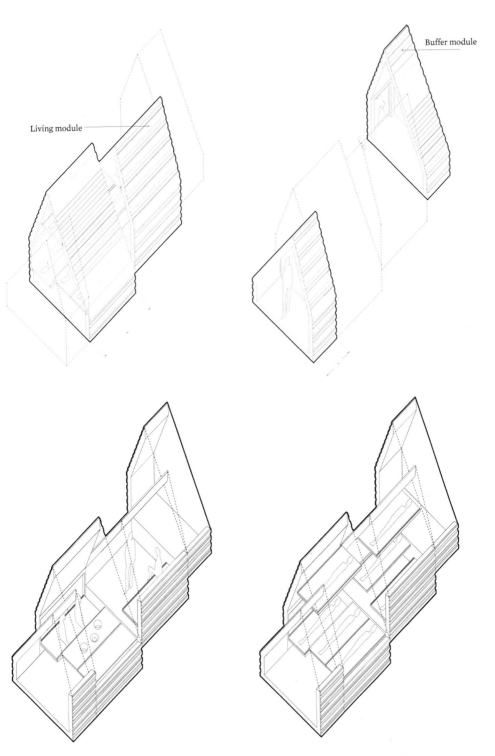

Living module

Buffer module

Frederick Kim, Katie MacDonald, Erin Pellegrino

Top: Module breakdown.   Bottom left: Social space.   Bottom right: Sleeping space.

The Cube

Xin Su

The Cube is a compact shelter including two levels, each of which contains four beds, arranged according to a pinwheel pattern. It both maximizes the efficiency of space and make space transferable between private and social uses. The structure is consistent with the logic of spatial elements. The detail, which is designed to adapt to the installation procedure, is carefully treated, so that all components could be prefabricated in a factory, transported to the site, and easily assembled there.

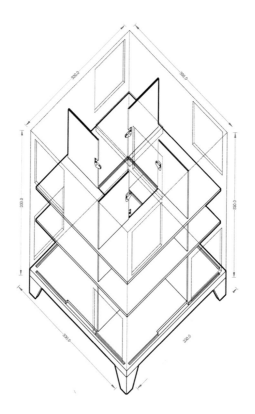

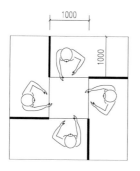
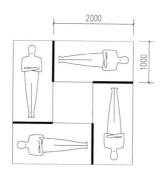
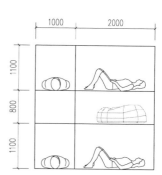

Top: Bed assembly.   Bottom: Habitation diagrams.

Connection systems.

Step Case

Frederick Kim
Katie MacDonald
Erin Pellegrino

Step Case is an economical, single-unit shelter that can exist as both a solitary unit and an assembly, conglomerating in a variety of configurations to adapt to various alpine slopes. Shaped by the human form, the shelter accommodates sleeping, sitting, and standing. A slide-out table and fold-out chair double as additional seating and shelving devices, providing a combination of pragmatism and flexible social space. With its stepped form, the roof becomes an extension of the mountain topography, allowing mountaineers to scale the building as well as gather and socialize in the warmer months.

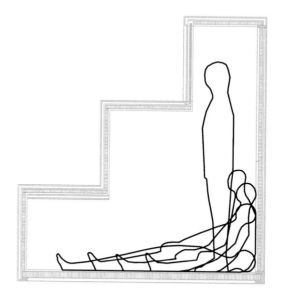

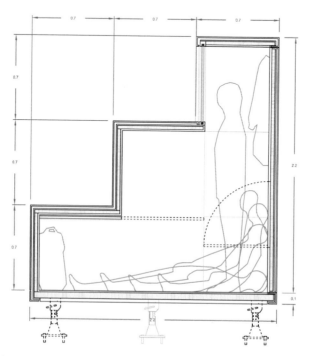

Stepped module assembly.

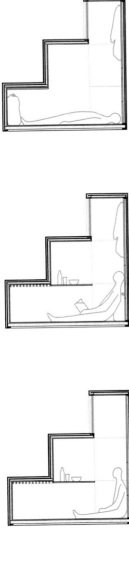

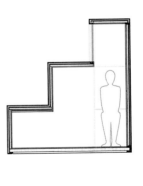

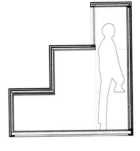

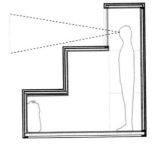

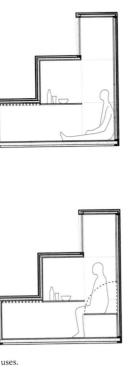

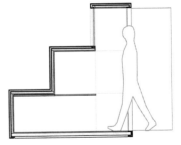

Varied spatial uses.

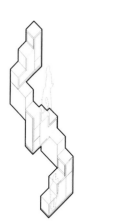

Step studies and models.

Frederick Kim, Katie MacDonald, Erin Pellegrino

43

Harmonika

Tianhang Ren

The shelter design is essentially an organic combination of a rotating and a folding structure. Instead of being static, the shelter derives from the perspectives of industrial design. By rotating two walls around the axis with beds attached to them, the shelter pushes the limits of materiality and space. It maximizes its versatility by changing the volume of interior space and offering multiple combinations with several units. The envelope of the shelter is inspired by the concertina, which resonates with the Slovenian traditional instrument, the harmonika. The concept of the envelope is functionally and culturally aligned with the Slovenian context.

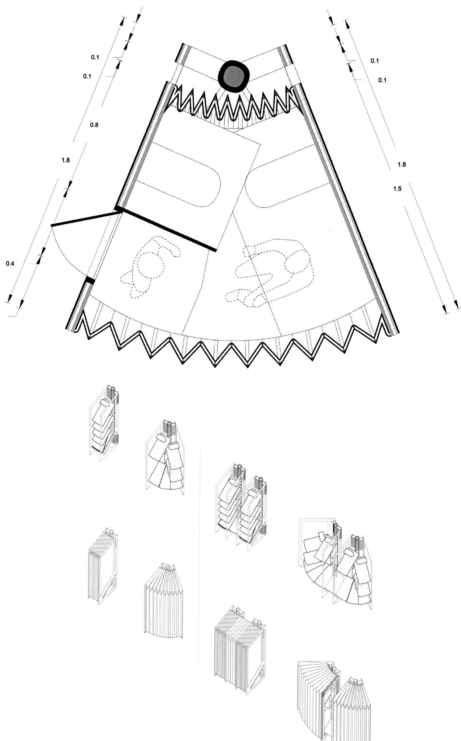

0.1
0.1
0.8
1.8
0.4

0.1
0.1
1.8
1.5

Top: Plan.

Bottom: Interior layouts.

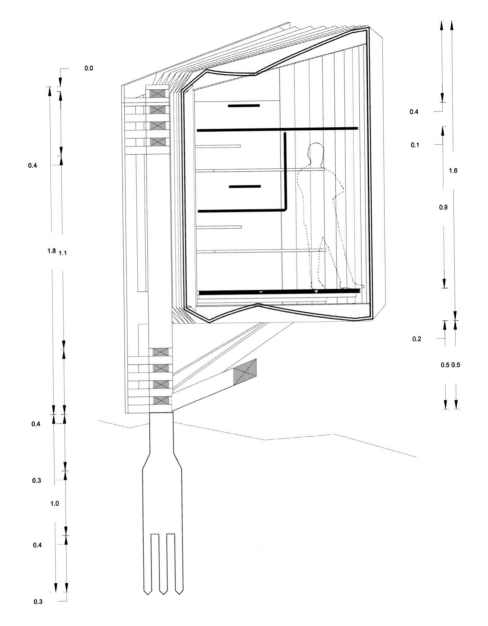

0.0

0.4

1.8 1.1

0.4

0.3

1.0

0.4

0.3

0.4

0.1

1.6

0.9

0.2

0.5 0.5

Section.

The Wind

Lauren McClellan

The Wind is a shelter composed of modules of the smallest possible inhabitable
unit that stack and turn about a central
social space. Each module is a planar
ring that thickens on one side to accommodate sleeping, sitting, standing, eating,
and circulating. The stacking aggregation
both defines the spiraling circulation and
gives the surfaces their dynamic character through their relationships.

    The following pages illustrate differ-
ent site and material tectonic realizations
of the shelter. One programmatic appoint-
ment of The Wind is inspired by Slovenian
bivaks and engenders a hiking shelter.
The round form and diagrid structure bear
extreme climatic loading (snow and wind).

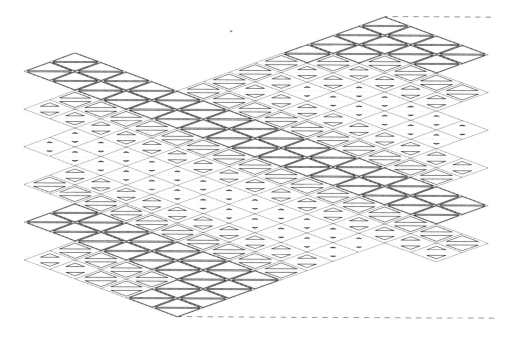

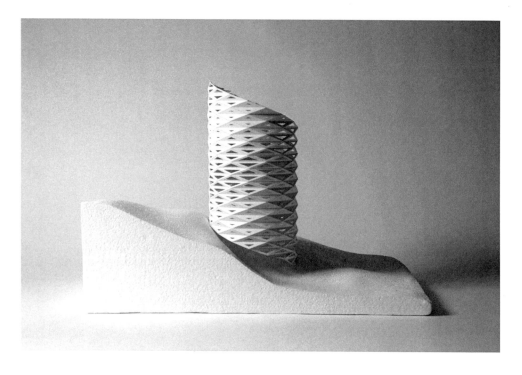

Top: Unfolded structural facade.   Bottom: Model.

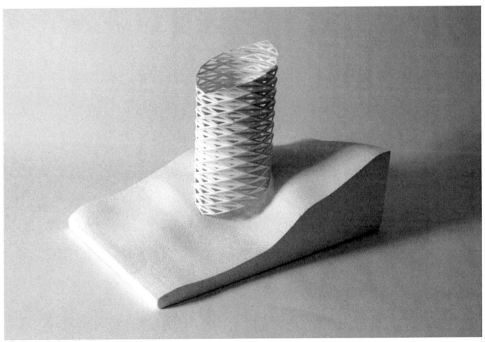

Model.

Interlock

Elizabeth Wu

Interlock is a modular unit that takes the traditional box-cut joint for wood-house construction to an extreme. The design explores how cross-laminated timber can be both a structural and thermal regulator while expressing the construction and interior programs through the facade. Using standard industry panel sizes and fabrication techniques of cutting and routing, the interlocking joint is updated to be integral to the *bivak* wall panels, allowing for streamlined construction and assembly at the factory.

For a more compact design and smaller footprint, the design conceptually interlocks the sleeping platforms by alternating the stacking orientation. Working with the alternating corner joints, each bed provides a strip window to offer views of the landscape and the environment. Privacy is maintained with this bed configuration while opening up a communal space over food prep counter. The design accommodates the unconventionally taller *bivak* structure by incorporating lateral struts to tie back to the mountain face while still remaining flexible enough to adapt to various inclines and topographies through means of adjustable feet. Additionally, the in situ orientation of the *bivak* can take advantage of the wind conditions and potential snow accumulation to provide pockets of protection at the unit entrance.

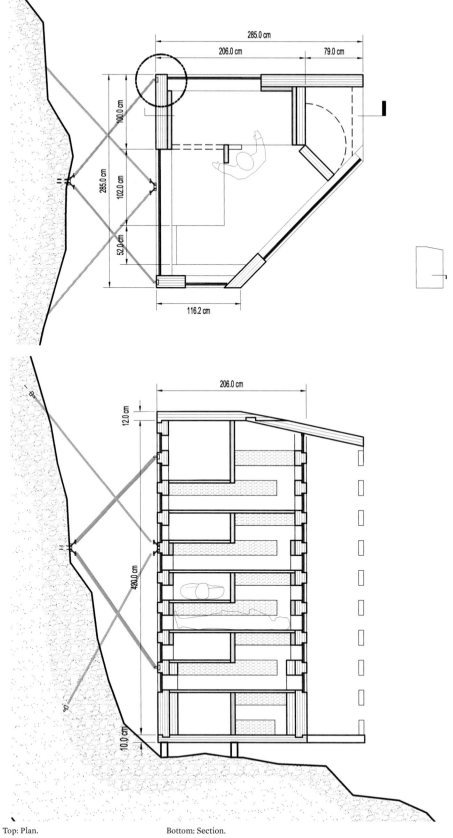

Interlock

Top: Plan.　　　　　　　　Bottom: Section.

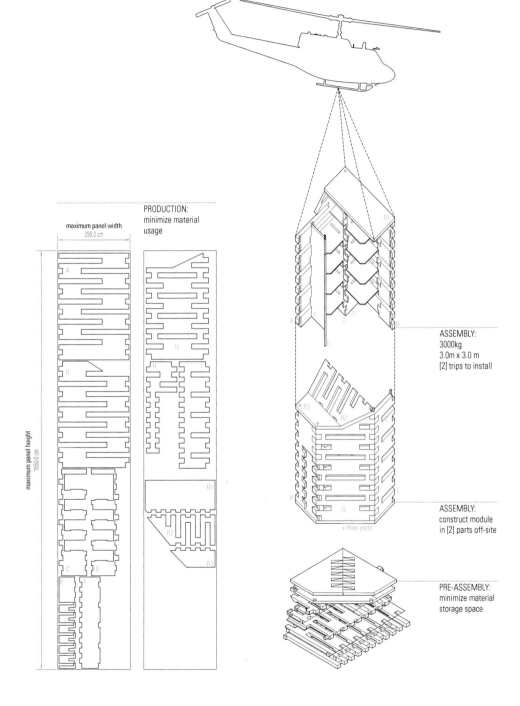

PRODUCTION:
minimize material
usage

maximum panel width
295.0 cm

maximum panel height
1650.0 cm

ASSEMBLY:
3000kg
3.0m x 3.0 m
[2] trips to install

ASSEMBLY:
construct module
in [2] parts off-site

+ floor plate

PRE-ASSEMBLY:
minimize material
storage space

Assembly diagrams.

Ledge House

Elizabeth Pipal

Ledge House is an eight-person shelter that seeks to distill the joy of the climbing experience while providing a brief respite from its sometimes too harsh reality. It hangs from a cliff, minimizing its impact on the natural landscape while simultaneously allowing spectacular views from within. Its seeming precariousness alludes to the adrenaline of mountaineering. It is a warm home for a moment of contemplation, before the climber forges on.

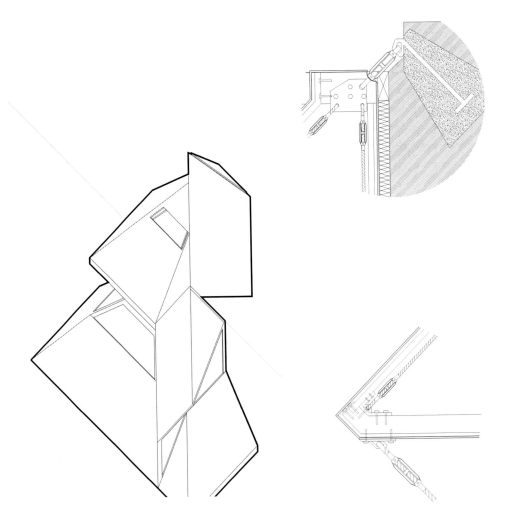

Connection details.

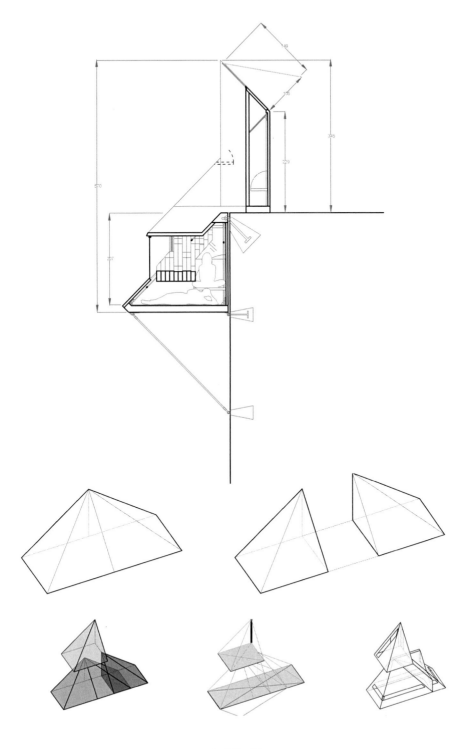

Top: Section.   Bottom: Spatial breakdown.

Extreme Adaptability

Oliver Bucklin

Through folding, this shelter transforms from a compact, stackable, easy-to-ship package to a fully inhabitable shelter in minutes. The built-in legs adapt to almost any slope, and the volume of the shelter almost triples in deployment.

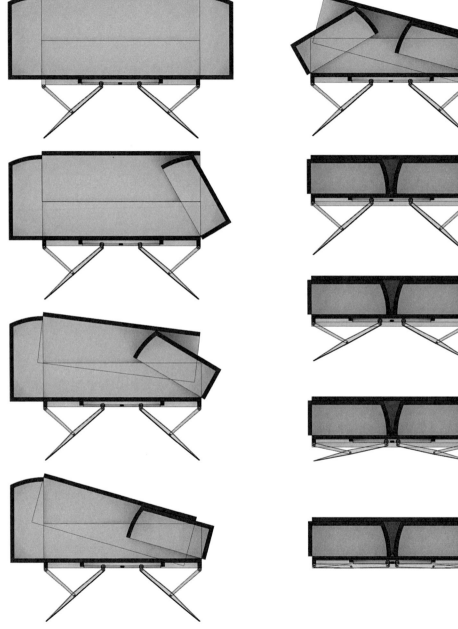

Unit unfolding.

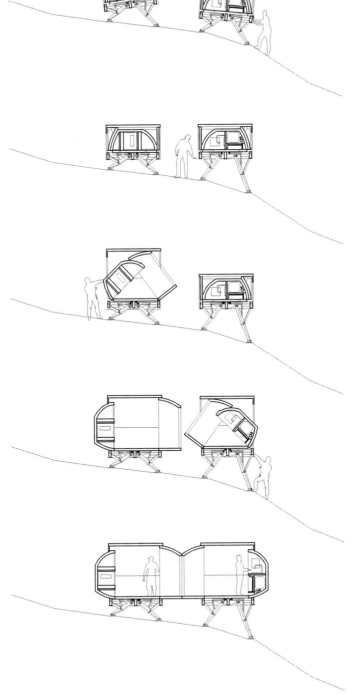

Unit aggregation.

Rotate

Myrna Ayoub

The main goal of this project was to create a multifunctional and easily changeable space for mountaineers seeking shelter. The prototype is inspired by the farmer's plow and its rotational mechanism. The interior space is organized through a module that rotates to become a seat, bed, storage, and counter space. The skin is fabricated from a series of ribs that mold to the rotation modules in cross section and are covered in translucent fiberglass textile coated in Teflon. The facade and modules are held by the Vierendeel truss structure, which allows the prototype to cantilever from the mountain.

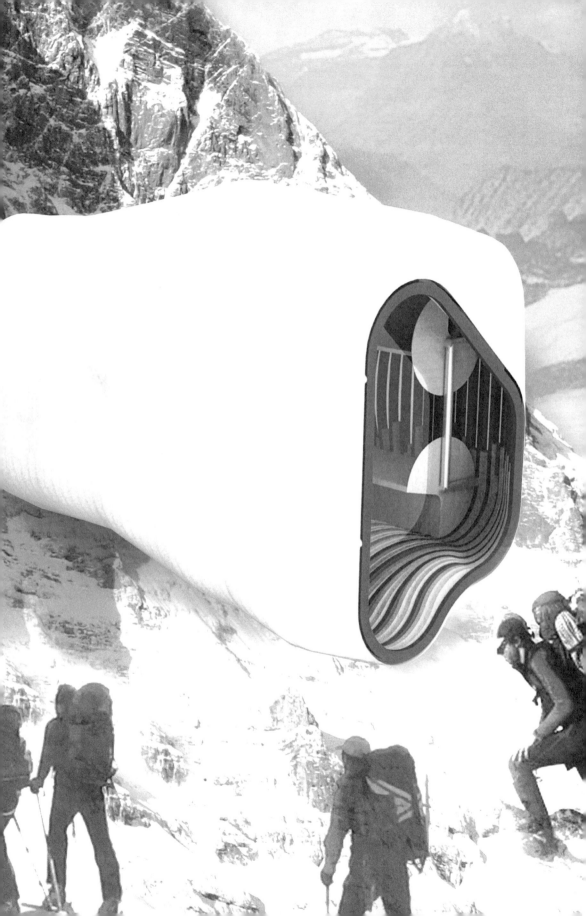

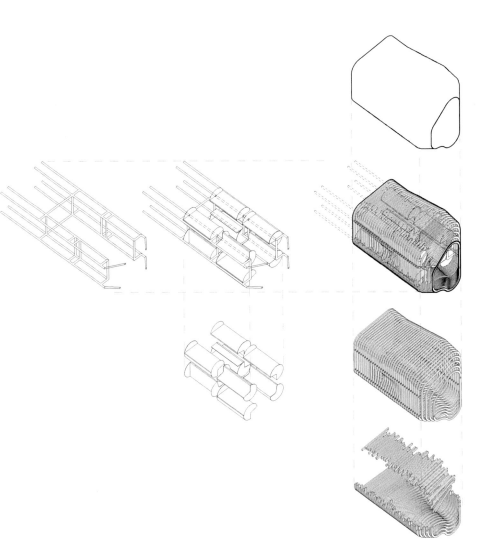

Rotate

Sectional views.

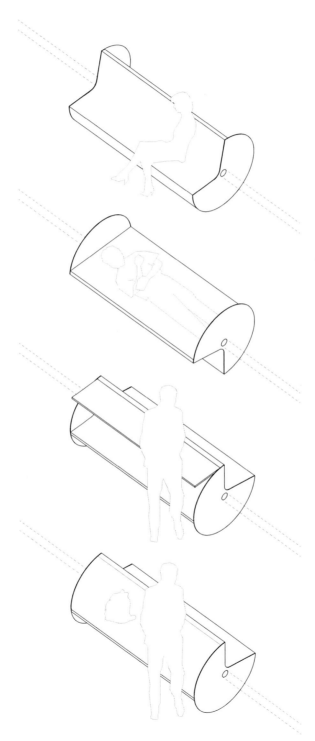

Rotating furniture element.

Tree House

Michael Meo

The Tree House is an ultralight, vertical safe haven for the hiker who loves to climb. The scheme organizes sleeping and storage spaces around a central circulation atrium. The pinwheel allows for the minimization of the interior volume while simultaneously maximizing each hiker's personal space. A hiker can experience connectivity with the other hikers occupying the Tree House while still being able to retreat to his or her own unique level and viewport within the tower. Each "L" bed unit has one leg for sleeping and another for storage of the hiker's personal gear. The outer form reflects the inner tectonic.

The Tree House is materially light. A tight weatherproof fabric stretches between the aluminum structural elements. The textile membrane decreases the shelter's thermal mass, allowing the heat from occupants to quickly warm the vertical volume.

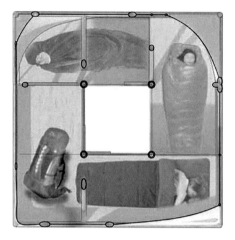

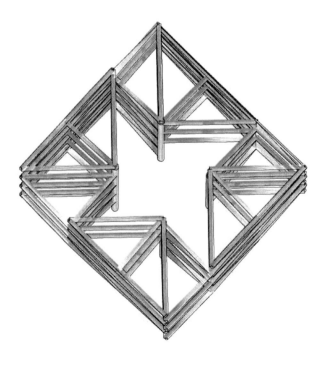

Top: Plan.   Bottom: Structure for transport.

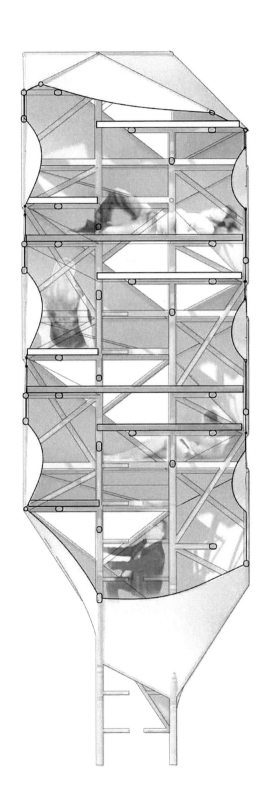

Section.

Aggregate: Alaska

In the second stage, the studio shifted focus from the peaks of Slovenia to the harsh climate of Alaska in the United States. In contemporary North America, there has been little effort to address varied environmental requirements of housing through architectural form. This tendency is magnified in the lack of consideration by Alaskan house builders of the extreme climate. Students used previous research and prototypes to further explore the significance of responsive design for housing accommodation within a larger-scale context.

Task

Challenge

Building on previous investigations and prototypes, students were challenged to use architecture to solve housing problems in Alaska. They chose a specific micro-location and designed housing to both accommodate the extreme climate and natural conditions and enhance an aspect of the community at a larger scale (economically, environmentally, etc.).

The architectural space had to stand resilient against difficult climate conditions and have no negative impact on the environment. It was important to respect the natural cycles and not alienate local populations.

In addition, due to high rates of population movement, the housing needed to be flexible to accommodate different population groups across changing residency seasons. This included the tourism and fish-processing industries in summer and legislative workers, mine workers, and university students during winter.

Housing Alaska

Klaus Mayer

The state of Alaska in the United States is ground zero for speculation on housing in extreme environments. Accelerated climate change has had a significant effect on Alaska's natural resources, shorelines, and geomorphology. This, combined with the harsh weather and limited access to rural areas, imposes new variables on every aspect of the design process. The challenges of these many environmental changes have brought to the forefront the importance of investigating, integrating, and expanding both existing and new sustainable technologies in construction and everyday living. Ultimately there is a real need for new housing developments. For that reason, our research on sustainable design and architecture carries with it a direct application, making it a perfect laboratory for looking at issues of energy efficiency, new materials, and evolving technologies.

The sheer vastness of the land in Alaska holds four distinct climatic zones: (1) maritime and (2) rainforest conditions along the coastline in southeast Alaska and the Aleutian chain; (3) the transitional zone and the continental zone of the interior; and (4) the semi-arid Arctic climate of the north slope. The vegetation that derives from these conditions is equally diverse, with the Pacific coastal forest ecoregion producing magnificent trees as tall as 200 feet along the coastlines of southeast Alaska and Kodiak Island. Most of Alaska's interior is part of the boreal forest that spans the majority of sub-Arctic regions. Farther north, we find ourselves in tundra-covered plains, leaving the trees behind. In the high Arctic region located above 66.5°N, inhabitants experience months without direct sunlight. In Barrow, for example, the sun sets on November 4 and does not rise again until January 23 (2012 calendar year). The opposite is true for the summer months, where the sun will not meet the horizon from May 10 to July 31. During this time, the temperature rises above 32 degrees Fahrenheit for a short and intense summer on the tundra. Nearly 85 percent of Alaska is situated on varying degrees of permafrost.

Alaska is a land of many extremes, including the ten tallest mountains in the United States. The temperature can swing from the record high of 100 degrees F at Fort Yukon (June 1915) to the record low of -80 degrees F in Prospect Creek (January 1971). The presence of more than 130 volcanoes as part of the "ring of fire" comes with fault lines that can generate daily earthquakes. The Good Friday earthquake of 1964 was the third-largest quake ever recorded, at 9.2 on the Richter scale. The impact and devastation was felt far beyond Alaska.

The land is very sparsely populated, with about 0.5 inhabitants per square kilometer. There are 736,732 (estimate for 2014) inhabitants in Alaska's 1,717,856 square kilometer area (which includes 13.77 percent water). Most of the population is located in south-central Alaska. The municipality of Anchorage surpassed 300,000 last summer. The second-largest population of about 100,000 is in Fairbanks's North Star borough, located 360 miles north of Anchorage. Juneau is the capital city and home to the third-largest community, with about 32,000 residents. Juneau is the only state capital in the United States that is not connected to the road system. Home to 229 federally recognized tribes, Alaska spans 3,639 kilometers east to west

and 2,285 kilometers north to south. Like the capital, most villages are connected only by air or boat, which has many consequences for logistics, especially for those in the construction industry.

Alaska has a long history of boom and bust. Natural resource extraction has always been at the core of this tendency, and the stories told about Alaska build up the myth of the exotic. Current reality television shows are carrying forth this tradition. State income derives largely

Whale bones utilized as structure.

from the oil industry through royalties and taxes, and attempts to diversify the economy have shown only marginal returns. Yet the state is well positioned to take advantage of many renewable resources.

Alaska's indigenous native community has a rich tradition of building appropriately for the environment. The long houses in southeast Alaska make use of the abundant timber. Roofs are slanted and have generous overhangs to protect from the drizzling rain. The houses of the Aleuts are mostly recessed into the land and thus out of the relentless rain and wind that can top 190 kilometers per hour. Summer dwellings for the interior traditionally consisted of a tentlike structure made from small willow trees covered with animal hide. These materials could be easily transported to the next location; the lifestyle was largely semi-nomadic as family units followed food sources.

The semi-subterranean winter dwelling of the Eskimo, in particular, is a great lesson in energy efficiency and resourcefulness. The location of the entrance, a long and tight tunnel, is dictated by the direction of the prevailing winds to ensure that it will not be covered by snow drifts that would block air flow and prevent access. Because the tunnel slopes down, it provides a place for the cold air to settle until it becomes warmer and rises into the main area. The support structure utilizes bones from the bowhead whale harvested earlier in the season. Sod covers the top of the dome over the main space. Above the cooking area is a small gut-skin skylight that also allows for smoke from the fire

to escape. The entire structure can be heated by the body heat of the occupants and a small seal-oil lamp. This structure is an example of the many lessons in understanding an environment and responding to it.

Alaska's current situation has presented new challenges as well as opportunities for designers to collaborate with communities experiencing a shortage of affordable housing. Prefabrication and new technologies are great research topics for places that are remote and have a small local labor pool. Population trends in Alaska indicate that many people are deciding to retire in the state, making senior housing a priority. Projects such as micro-housing, hotels, spas, and visitor centers can fill a gap in the existing offerings.

With climate conditions changing all over Alaska, it is not only housing that deserves research. Twelve villages have been identified as in need of relocation due to coastal erosion or other environmental factors such as rising sea levels. The potential for great design is real and good ideas are desperately needed. If we are successful in our pursuit, we can apply our research to many regions and set an example for the future of sustainable design and architecture, especially in the harsh environments of the Arctic.

Use of animal skins as cladding.
Skinhouse and Inuit, St. Lawrence Bay, Siberia, 1922.

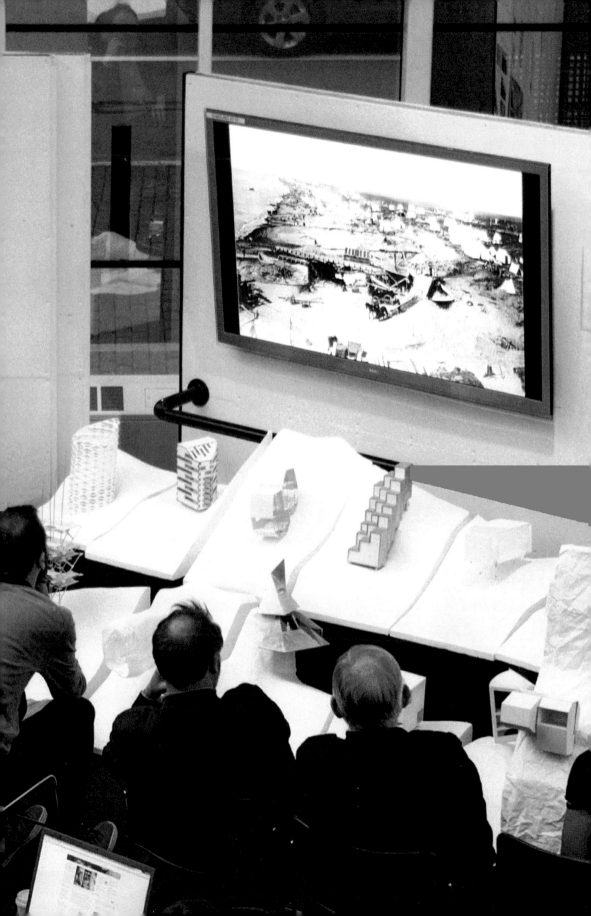

Home Away from Home

Myrna Ayoub
Nadia Perlepe

This project evolved from research about Alaska and its rich heritage of fishing— its effect on the growth of cities and the economy of the state. The proposed site of Unalaska and Dutch Harbor is the leading commercial fishing port in the nation. In a city with a population of 4,200, there are 36,000 seasonal workers. Given the influx of workers during the fishery seasons, we propose a housing project that instills a new way of living. The city of Unalaska is currently undertaking a housing initiative, and the need for increased quality and affordable housing is of utmost importance for the city. The goal of the proposal is to create a development that could be easily constructed and transported to such a remote location. The unit is adopted from the original *bivak* studies that created an amphitheatrical interior unit from half of a shipping container. Each container is connected by a joint that acts as the communal space for the workers. This system is explored in two developments: a sloped mountain overlooking Dutch Harbor and a flat site adjacent to the main city center. The aggregation of these joints and units explores spaces that provide a connection with nature through beautiful views and create courtyard pockets for various programs. These supplemental programs serve as spaces of interaction for seasonal workers and locals, blurring boundaries between the populations. These interactions promote communication, tolerance, and an understanding of culture. The aim of this development is to create a "home away from home" for seasonal workers—a home of comfort, quality, and community.

container	container/2	2 units	1 unit	our unit	**OUR UNIT !**
40' x 8' | 12m x 2.4m	20' x 8' | 6m x 2.4m	20' x 8' | 6m x 2.4m	20' x 8' | 6m x 2.4m	20' x 8' | 6m x 2.4m	20' x 8' | 6m x 2.4m

EXTREME FORCES | wind, sun, snow, views

snow	sun	views	wind
roof slope 5'	energy efficiency / smart roof		unit rotation

UNIT + JOINT | home away from home

 + =

units	joint	home away from home

JOINTS | communal spaces

2 UNIT JOINT
2-4 workers

GATHER

EAT

3 UNIT JOINT
4-6 workers

ENJOY

PLAY

EAT

3 UNIT JOINT
4-6 workers

ENJOY

PLAY

EAT

4 UNIT JOINT
12 workers

GATHER

EAT

PLAY

Formal explorations of orientation and joinery.

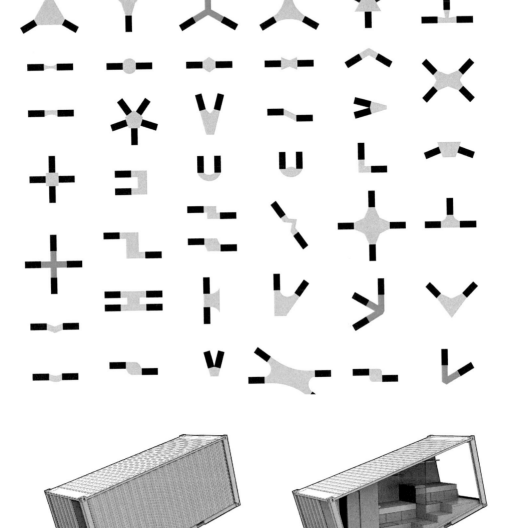

Top: Connection diagrams.   Bottom: Shipping container and interior.

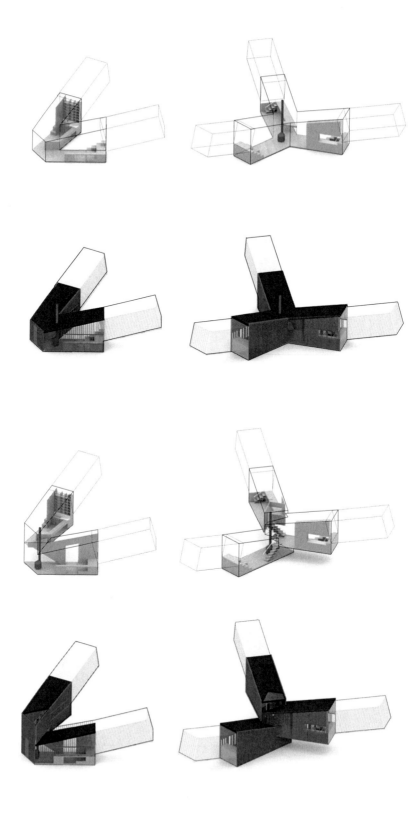

Formal explorations of orientation and
joinery.

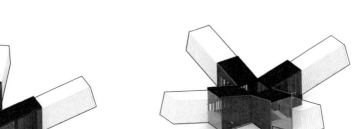

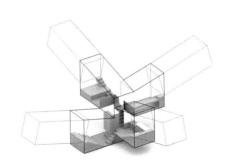

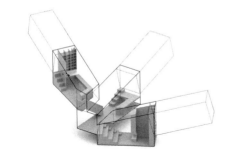

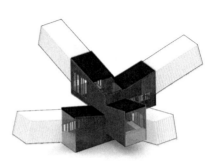

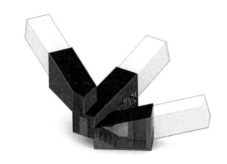

Myrna Ayoub, Nadia Perlepe

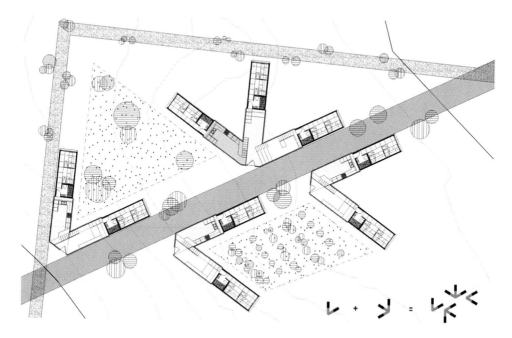

Topographical scheme for housing
module deployment.

Myrna Ayoub, Nadia Perlepe

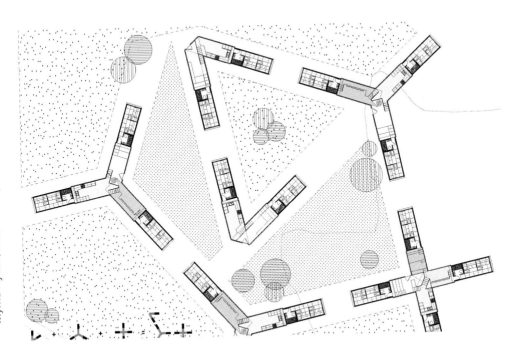

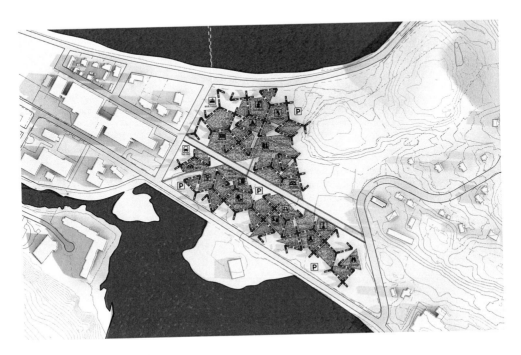

Flat scheme for housing module
deployment.

Top: Exterior perspective.   Bottom left and right: Interior view.

Aging in Place

Elizabeth Pipal
Xin Su
Elizabeth Wu

Alaska faces a shifting population demographic in the near future. Currently one of the youngest states in the United States, it has the distinction of having one of the fastest growing elderly populations (65-plus age bracket). As elsewhere across the United States, the housing supply in the city of Anchorage has not been able to keep up with the growing demand for more multigenerational living.

In considering housing in extreme environments, our group attempts to address the need for more flexible living conditions that would allow families to grow and stay connected. The aging-in-place model of living emphasizes staying linked to neighbors and familiar associations. The proposed types of housing units provide for senior couples, families just starting out, and multigenerational households in a communal setting.

Our site is located in the vicinity of Centennial Village, a senior living complex administered by the Cook Inlet Housing Authority. Situated on the slopes of Joint Base Elmendorf-Richardson, the site offers an opportunity to link senior housing back to the landscape while still staying connected to urban living. The site strategy considers hydrological flows and potential snow accumulation points to position unit clusters. Linkages between units offer both views of landscape and places for neighbors to interact.

The topography and climate of a mountainous site allowed for an exploration of the ramp typology within each residential unit. The ramps adapt to terrain changes while also becoming a central physical means of extending the landscape into living areas. One of the design challenges of building in Alaska is accounting for limited access to daylight. The circulation ramps are situated to take advantage of most direct sunlight hours; the facade pattern and stepped unit positioning allow for interior gardens along this major circulation path. These moments where nature meets built environment offer a place for families to gather and share time and space.

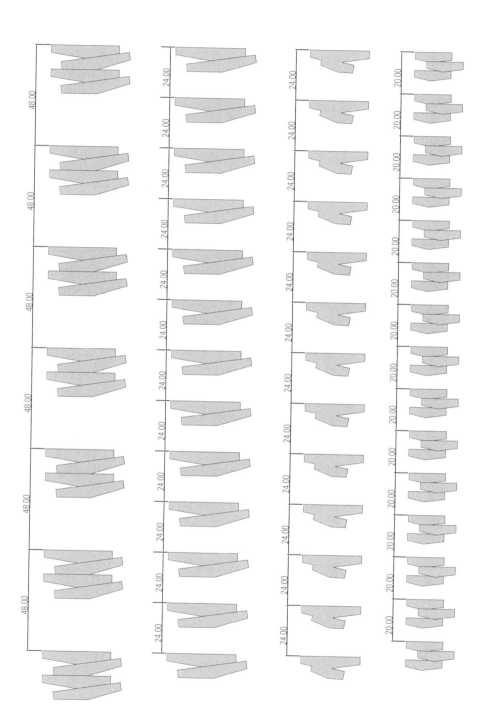

Formal aggregation studies.

Elizabeth Pipal, Xin Su, Elizabeth Wu

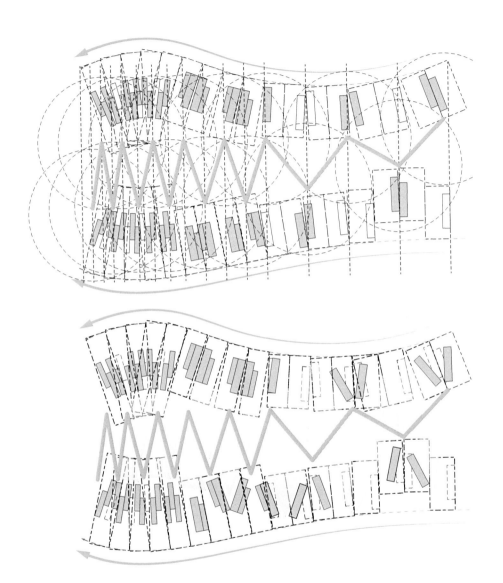

Site plan.

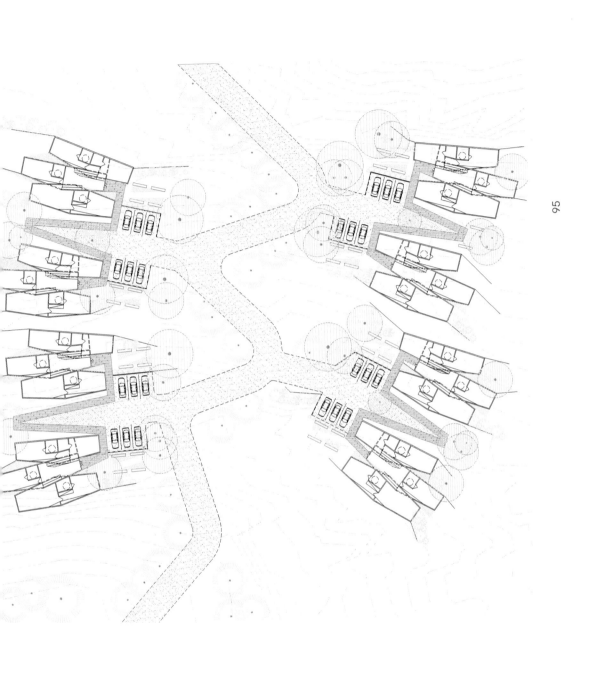

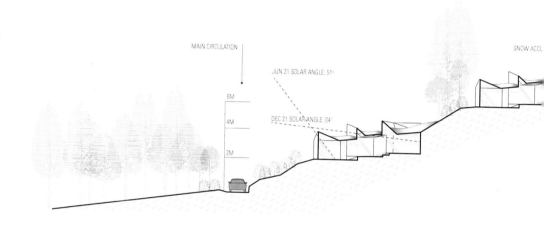

MAIN CIRCULATION

JUN 21 SOLAR ANGLE: 51°

DEC 21 SOLAR ANGLE: 04°

SNOW ACCL

6M

4M

2M

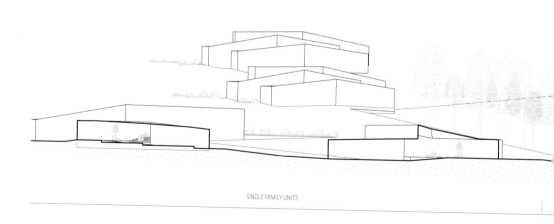

SINGLE FAMILY UNITS

Top and bottom: Site section.

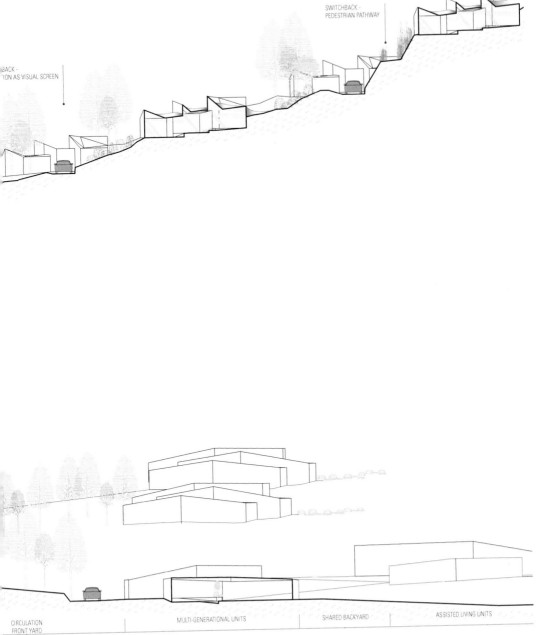

SWITCHBACK -
PEDESTRIAN PATHWAY

BACK -
TION AS VISUAL SCREEN

CIRCULATION
FRONT YARD

MULTI-GENERATIONAL UNITS

SHARED BACKYARD

ASSISTED LIVING UNITS

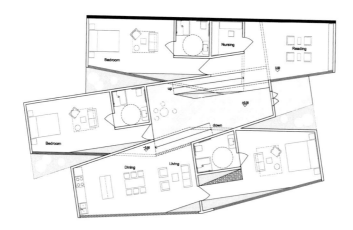

Top: Cross section.

Bottom: Plan.

Elizabeth Pipal, Xin Su, Elizabeth Wu

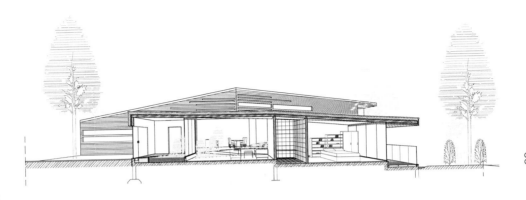

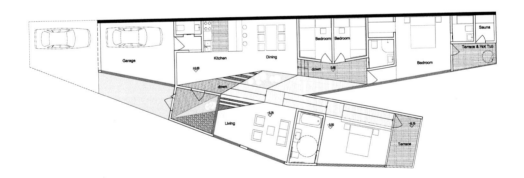

Top: Longitudinal section.   Bottom: Plan.

House Hotel Hut

Frederick Kim
Katie MacDonald
Erin Pellegrino

The transition from indigenous to Western control of Alaska has transformed the culture, economy, and architecture of the region from a nomadic, trade-based civilization housed in temporal, communal structures into a series of permanent, industrial cities articulated by generic suburban homes. Today, Alaska's uprooted native populations are still dealing with the aftermath and face issues of poverty, powerlessness, and cultural fragmentation. Replacing a landscape of igloos, tents, fish racks, and communal housing, native homes today are largely government-funded, cheaply constructed, Western-style single-family homes whose designs fail to adequately acknowledge the specific challenges of the Alaskan climate, including seasonal transformation, community, daylighting, and coldness.

House Hotel Hut adapts vernacular thermodynamic strategies of temporal ice architecture into the design of permanent social housing for the uprooted native populations of Birch Lake, Fairbanks, Alaska.Traditional elements of the Alaskan igloo—the entrance vestibule, the sleeping niche, and the centralized fire—are recomposed into a vertical configuration centered on the hearth, with eating and living niches on the bottom floor.

House Hotel Hut proposes a new economic model and housing typology tailored to the local vernacular architecture and fishing economy. Because of both the vocational and recreational economic potential of ice fishing, the complex aggregates three scales of habitation: (I) the single-family home, (2) the mobile tourist cabin, and (3) the deployable fishing shanty. The resulting three interlocking volumes expand during summer, providing rental lakeside cabins and shanties to tourists as well as hospitality income to homeowners. During the colder months, the houses and hotel units contract back together, minimizing surface area and reducing heating costs. The shanties are free to deploy onto the ice, allowing both the local fishing industry and tourist fishing rentals to generate income. Each building is centered on a chimney, providing radiant heating. Ample light enters through a glass facade, fragmented by aluminum fins that modulate light.

Integrating permanent housing for local fishermen, temporary housing for tourists, and ice-fishing shanties for vocational and recreational use, the complex synthesizes multiple users and the cyclical transformation of the local economy. The resulting housing provides protection against the cold, creates a new model of communal living, and stimulates economic growth.

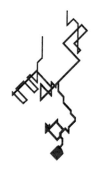

Chimney

Furniture

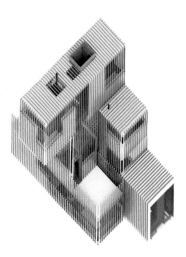

Aggregation

House

Frederick Kim, Katie MacDonald, Erin Pellegrino

Walls

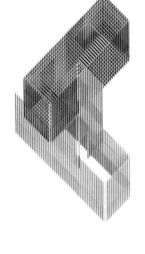

Skin

Hotel cabin

Ice fishing hut

Top: Summer deployment of hotel
cabin. Bottom, following page: Winter
contraction of hotel cabin into house and
deployment of ice hut onto lake.

Top: Winter contraction of hotel cabin into house and deployment of ice hut onto lake. Bottom, following page: Summer deployment of hotel cabin.

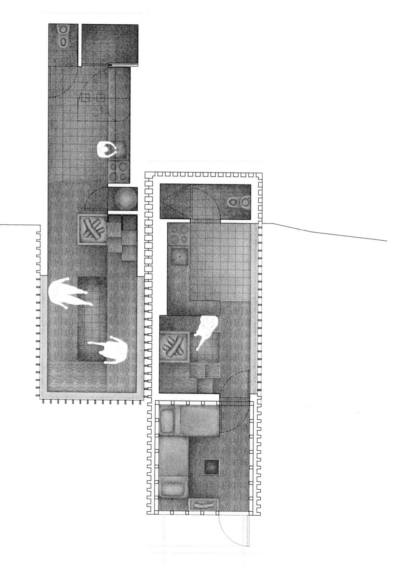

Plan, level one.

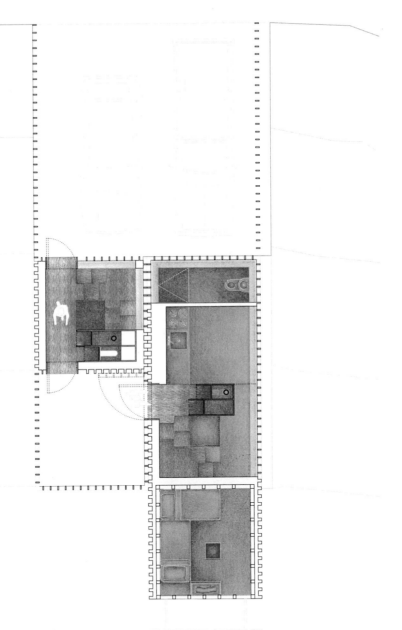

Plan, level two.

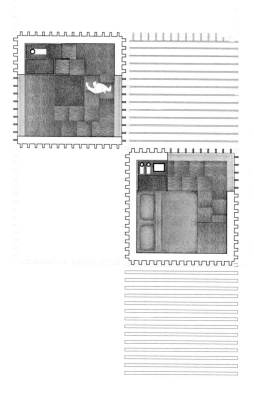

Plan, level three.

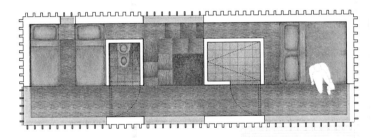

Plan, level four.

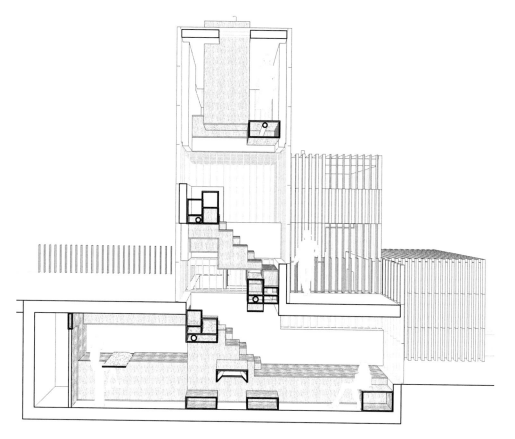

Perspectival sections through hearth of
building.

Frederick Kim, Katie MacDonald, Erin Pellegrino

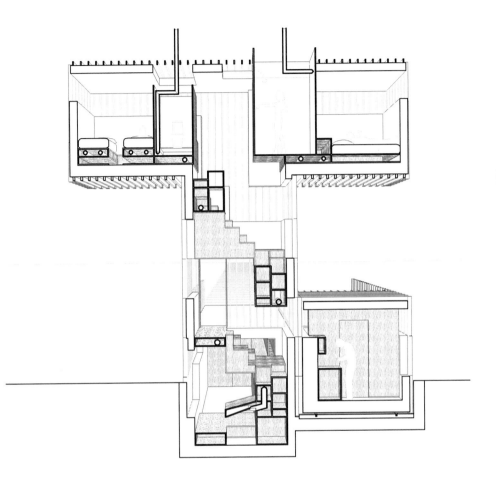

Alaska House

Zheng Cui

Alaska, a unique destination, is loved by adventurers as well as culture enthusiasts. Tourism has been a dominant economic force since the late 1960s, and Alaska has warmly welcomed large numbers of tourists, with steady growth over the last decade. Ice fishing, dog sledding, wildlife viewing, volcano observation, and multi-sport adventures have become the most popular things to do in Alaska. This project proposes a business idea that provides online ordering of portable housing and offers delivery and set-up service for tourists across the state.

The housing modules are made of local wood and lightweight thermal mass materials. They are compact and light enough to transport through Alaska via railway, ship, road transportation, airship, or icemobile. The modules can be transferred into tourist camps, research stations in the natural environment, or varied module aggregations in the urban context. The modules could be used as row houses, hotels, or public event space for seasonal workers, local governments, or other organizations. The module aggregation can be disassembled after use and transported back to the storage location for the next round of online ordering. The aim of this development is to create freedom for adventurers exploring Alaska.

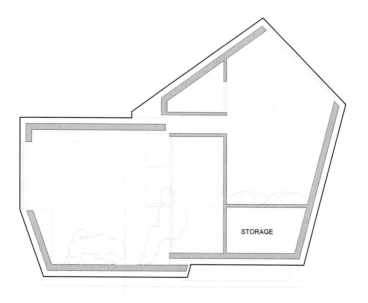

STORAGE

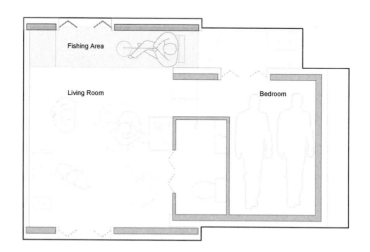

Fishing Area

Living Room

Bedroom

Module.

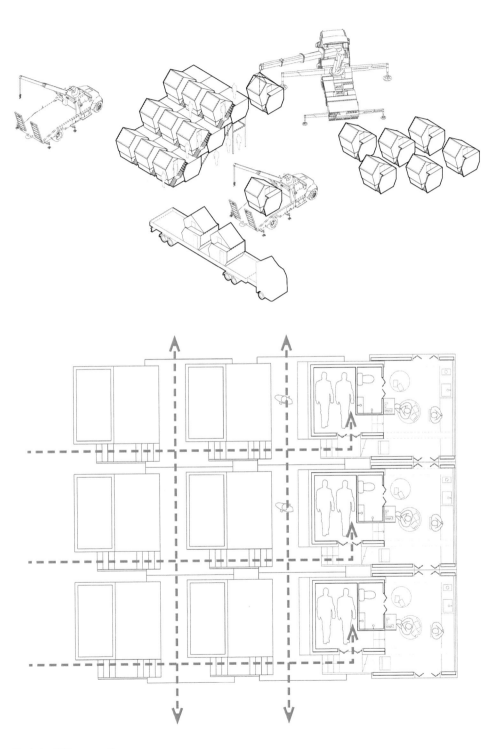

Tourist ice-fishing aggregation.

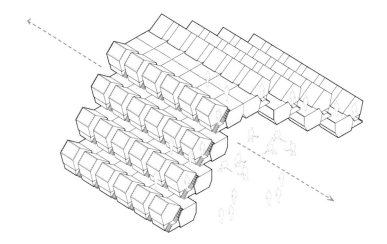

Aggregation strategies.

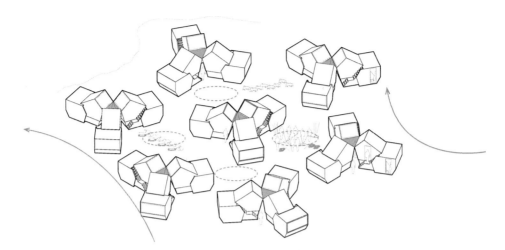

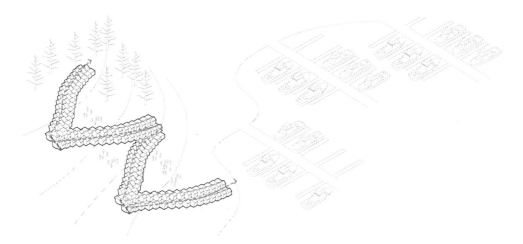

Top: Site plan.   Bottom: Model.

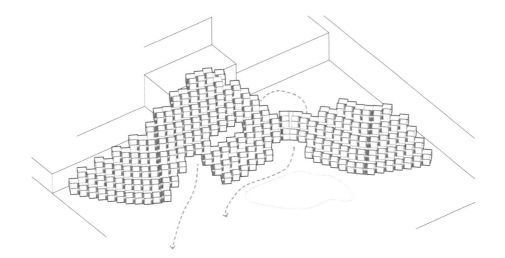

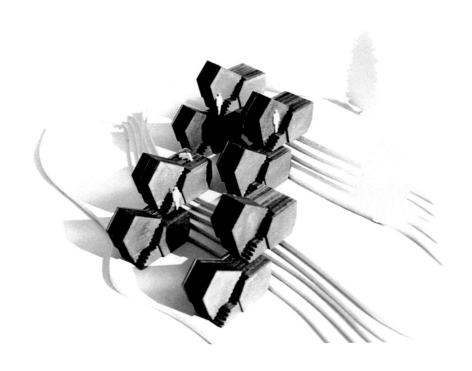

Top: Site plan.   Bottom: Model.

Hydrothermal Resort

Lauren McClellan

The Wind *bivak* is the inspiration and preliminary model of self-sufficiency and structural integration for the design of a resort on Umnak Island, Alaska. The design proposal realizes Umnak Island as a destination for extreme tourism—the idea being to invite and accommodate those excited by the geographically, geologically, and climatically extreme site. The resort is comprised of cabins, central lodges, dining, and transportation to/from various viewpoints, hunting/fishing grounds, and hydrothermal activity.

Open year-round, weather-tight, plumbed, and furnished cabins would be maintained by guides and accommodate up to six people each. The development would be entirely wind powered and geothermally heated. All-terrain vehicles would provide transportation for gear from the docks and airstrips to the cabins.

Umnak Island has hot springs, steaming beaches, and geysers. The resort would also provide world-class marine mammal viewing and birding, especially between Dutch Harbor and Umnak Island. The island has a rich Aleut history dating back 12,000 years, combined with the modern ranching, fishing, and military history of the region.

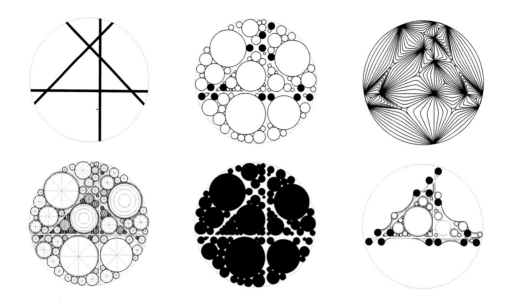

Top: Plans.

Bottom: Model details.

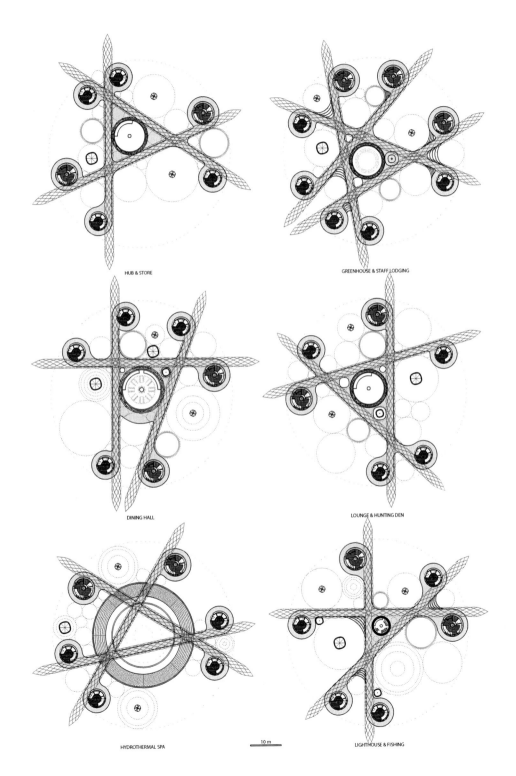

HUB & STORE

GREENHOUSE & STAFF LODGING

DINING HALL

LOUNGE & HUNTING DEN

HYDROTHERMAL SPA

10 m

LIGHTHOUSE & FISHING

GEOT

Geothermal heating strategy.

Tree / House

Michael Meo

Located 60 miles off the coast of Nome, Alaska, King Island is a mountainous sanctuary home to a village abandoned 50 years ago. Only several square kilometers, this small island is entirely mountainous. In the early 1900s, the village of Ukivok was home to nearly 200 Ukivokmiut. A migratory people, the Ukivokmiut would spend winters on the island, hunting whales and walruses while foraging for berries on the land. Summers were spent near mainland Nome carving and farming. When the state government moved King Island's only school to the mainland in 1960, so too had to move the youth. Without the participation of the youth in everyday subsistence activities, the elders could no longer sustain their way of life, and by 1966 the entire village was abandoned.

This Tree / House agglomeration seeks to create a transgenerational cultural bridge between the displaced Ukivokmiut people and their ancestral land. The island is just far enough to make a one-day trip impossible. At the periphery of the village, the Tree / House provides a safe and culturally resonant shelter for visitors to stay overnight. The canvas-clad Tree / House is a modern adaption of the stilt-based walrus-skin huts that still adorn the island. The structures can grow and interface seamlessly at their connecting nodes. Flexible, lightweight, contextually relevant, and scalable, the Tree / House opens a new bridge across disparate geographies and a migratory culture.

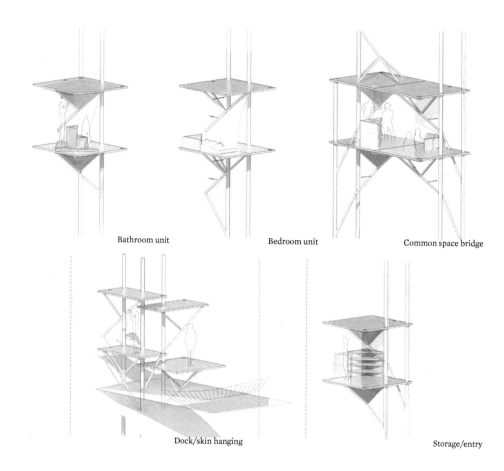

Bathroom unit   Bedroom unit   Common space bridge

Dock/skin hanging   Storage/entry

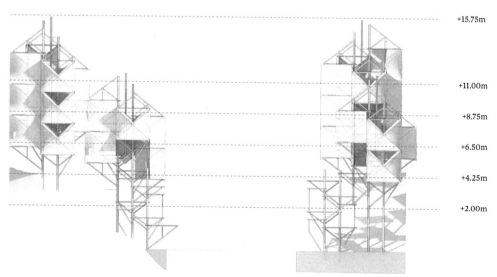

+15.75m

+11.00m

+8.75m

+6.50m

+4.25m

+2.00m

Bathroom unit

Dock/skin hanging

Bedroom unit

Common space bridge

Storage/entry

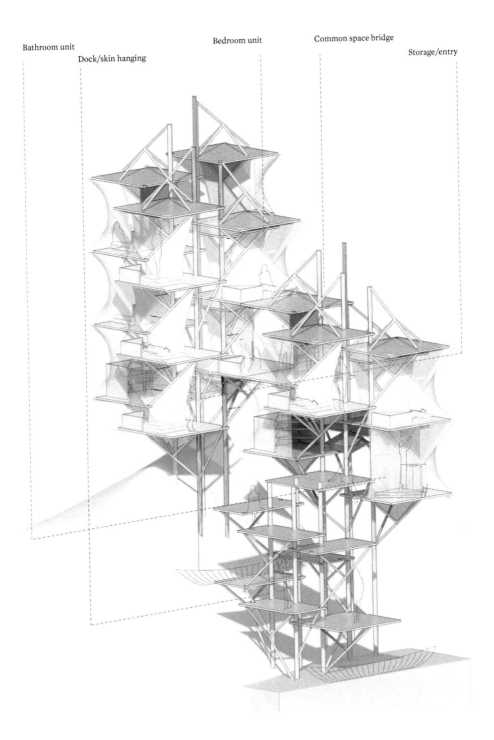

Aggregation of units.

Housing in Alaska

Tianhang Ren

Continuing the idea of the folding struc-ture in the *bivak* design, this housing project takes up the systematic aggrega-tion and combination of the modules. The single module is an evolution of the pre-vious *bivak* design, keeping the essence of foldable structure and translating the philosophy of simplicity into the aggre-gation. The basic module consists of one fixed room and one set of expandable (in-flatable) ETFE membranes, which is very cost-effective for the clients. By putting modules together, the aggregation can follow varied patterns. The expandable ETFE membranes maintain the versa-tility of the house, making it adaptive to occupants' needs by creating or remov-ing rooms. All of the elements combined contribute to the dynamics and flexibility that housing projects rarely have, which is crucial for vacation houses.

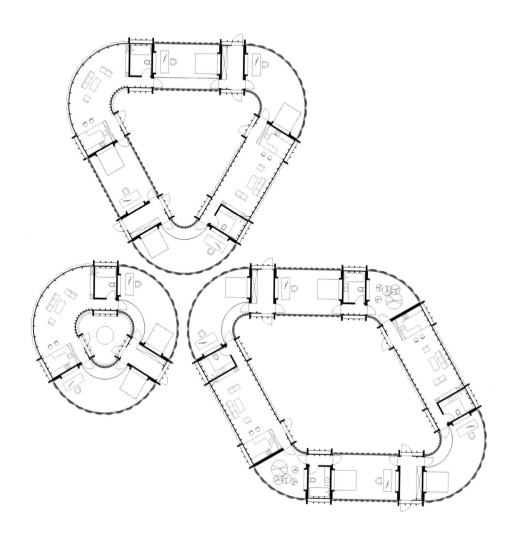

Plan: Various arrangements.

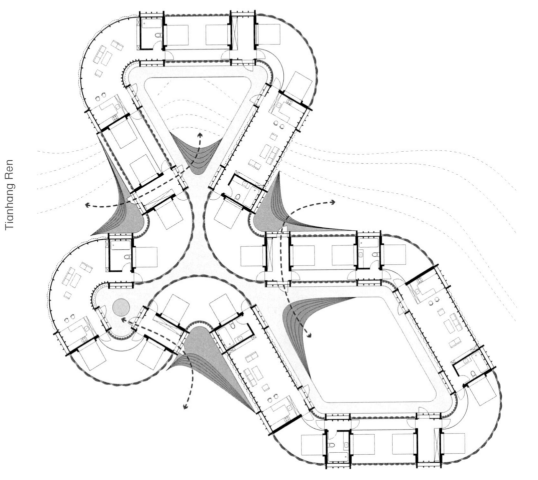

Plan: Connection possibilities.

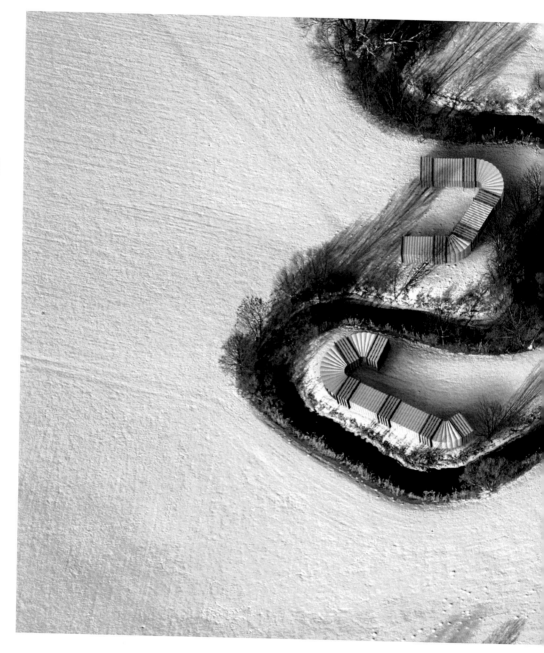

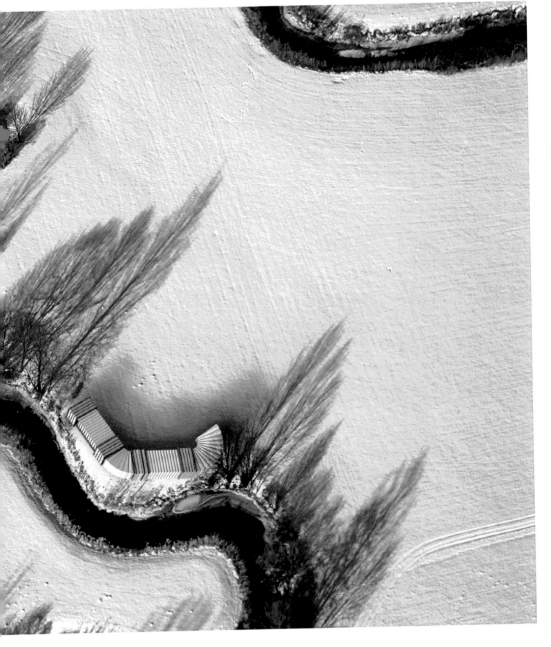

Research Station

Oliver Bucklin

Nesting volumes offers a means to
create an expandable structure that
can accomodate a population in flux.
By nesting building members, spaces
can expand and new program elements
can be created with simple movements.
When spaces are unused, the volumes
create redundant layers of insulation.
In Antarctica, this means that energy will
not be wasted heating unused building
volume, and extra layers will make for
more efficient insulation during times of
lowest occupancy, typically during the
coldest months.

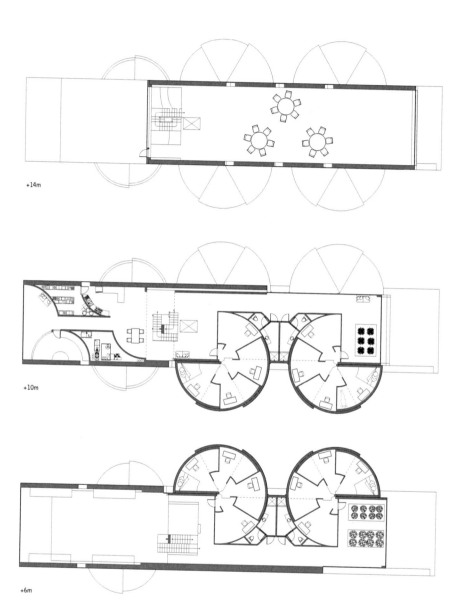

+14m

+10m

+6m

Plans: Deployed.

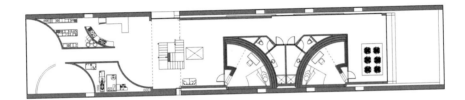

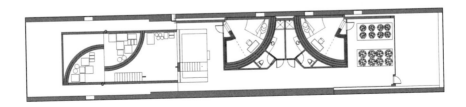

Plan: Compacted.

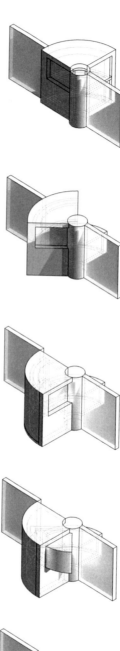

Joint detail.

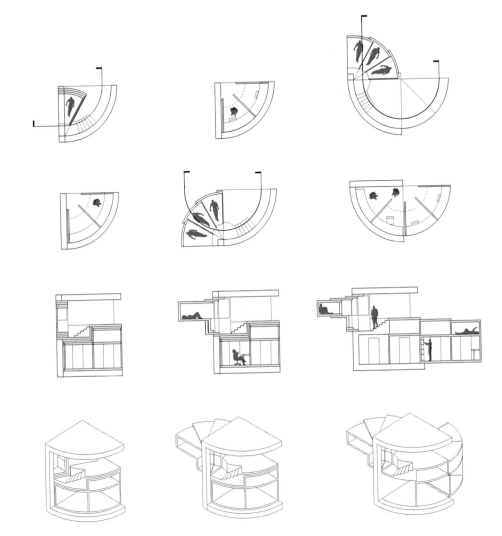

Top: Plan of unfolded space.   Middle: Section of unfolded space.   Bottom: Isometric of unfolded space.

Rok Oman and Spela Videcnik are graduates of the Ljubljana School of Architecture and London's Architectural Association. They established OFIS arhitekti in 1996 after winning several prominent competitions, including those for Maribor Football Stadium and Ljubljana City Museum. Many of their projects have been nominated for the Mies van der Rohe Award, and they were nominated for the Chernikhov Prize. Among their awards are a Silver IOC/IAKS medal for their football stadium (2009), the European Grand Prix for Innovation Award (2006), and the British Young Architect of the Year Award. In 2010 their Farewell Chapel was selected as religious object of the year by *ArchDaily*, and in 2013 they received the Plecnik Award for Space Wheel Center.

Over the past 10 years they have been working with national and international clients from the private, commercial, and governmental sectors. Their built projects range from low-budget housing to private designs and include museums, stadiums, and apartments.

Based in Ljubljana, the practice operates internationally, taking part in competitions and architectural discourse worldwide. Built projects include a business complex in Venice Marghera, Italy (2008), and a residential complex in Graz, Austria (2001). After winning a competition for a design of 180 apartments in Petit Ponts, Paris, they opened a branch office in France in 2007. This was followed by a second large-scale development, a football stadium in Borisov, Belarus, that opened in 2014.

The concept of the option studio derived from the inspiration of traditional architecture. The goal was to inspire young architects to develop a unique architectural language that creates context by engaging with the surrounding environment.

Hanif Kara

combines practice with teaching, currently as Professor in Practice of Architectural Technology at the Harvard University Graduate School of Design. He is a fellow of the Royal Institute of British Architects, the Institution of Civil Engineers, the Royal Academy of Engineering, the Institution of Structural Engineers, and the Royal Society for the Encouragement of Arts, Manufactures, and Commerce (RSA). Kara is on the board of trustees of the Architecture Foundation, is a former member of the Commission for Architecture and the Built Environment, and is a past member of the Design for London Advisory Group to the Mayor of London.

As Design Director and cofounder of AKT II, his particular "design-led" approach and interest in innovative form, material uses, and complex analysis methods have allowed him to work on numerous award-winning projects.

His published works include *Design Engineering* (2008), a retrospective of AKT's first decade, *Interdisciplinary Design: New Lessons from Architecture and Engineering* (2012), and *Deliverance of Design: Making, Mending, and Revitalising Structures* (2013), on the works of AKT II from 1996 to 2018.

Klaus Mayer

is principal of Klaus Mayer Freier Architect, based in Anchorage, Alaska, and Berlin. He received his degree in architecture from the University of Applied Science in Stuttgart, Germany. He has lived and worked in Alaska since 1995. From 2001 to 2013, he was co-founder and partner of Mayer Sattler-Smith. Mayer was appointed trustee of the Alaska Design Forum in 1998, and from 1999 to 2012 was president of the board. He was a Loeb Fellow at the Harvard University Graduate School of Design for the academic year 2004–2005.

In 2006 Mayer was part of a team that won the local housing competition for Cook Inlet housing, for an "ideal house." Other works such as the "house for a musher" have received local and regional AIA honor awards. He is a frequent guest critic at Harvard University, the Massachusetts Institute of Technology, the University of Michigan, and the University of Munich among others. He teaches sustainability in the built environment at the University of Alaska, Anchorage.

Colophon

Habitation in Extreme Environments
Instructors
Rok Oman, Spela Videcnik
Report Editors
Katie MacDonald, Erin Pellegrino
Report Design
Katie MacDonald, Erin Pellegrino

A Harvard University Graduate
School of Design Publication
**Dean and Alexander and Victoria
Wiley Professor of Design**
Mohsen Mostafavi
Assistant Dean for Communications
Benjamin Prosky
Editor in Chief
Jennifer Sigler
Senior Editor
Melissa Vaughn
Associate Editor
Leah Whitman-Salkin
Publications Coordinator
Meghan Sandberg

Series design by Laura Grey and Zak Jensen

ISBN 978-1-934510-48-3

Copyright © 2015, President and Fellows
of Harvard College. All rights reserved. No
part of this book may be reproduced in any
form without prior written permission from the
Harvard University Graduate School of Design.

Acknowledgments
We would like to thank Dean and Alexander
and Victoria Wiley Professor of Design Mohsen
Mostafavi and Architecture Department Chair
Iñaki Ábalos for the opportunity to teach this
studio, Hanif Kara and Wolfgang Rieder for
their support and contributions, and Klaus
Mayer for his important input. We are grateful
to Anze Cokl with PD Jesenice for offering us a
real site and trusting us to build a real shelter.
Thanks also to all of the students for their
hard work during the studio and in preparing
the Harvard GSD exhibition and this book.
We appreciate the critics for their important
words during pinups and jury review. Finally,
a special thanks to the OFIS team: Andrej
Gregoric, Vanessa Abram, Jamie Lee, and
Jade Manbodh.

Image Credits
Cover: Katie MacDonald and Erin Pellegrino.
page 9: © chripell.
page 12, clockwise from top left: © brewbooks,
Lacen, Mark Stevens, chripell, David Edgar,
and chripell
page 78: Lomen Bros.
pages 132–33; 136–37: © Klaus Leidorf (www.
leidorf.de)

The editors have attempted to acknowledge all
sources of images used and apologize for any
errors or omissions.

Harvard University
Graduate School of Design
48 Quincy Street
Cambridge, MA 02138

publications@gsd.harvard.edu
gsd.harvard.edu

25598239R00084

Made in the USA
San Bernardino, CA
04 November 2015